Gaza Narrates Poetry

Ahmed Miqdad

Copyright © 2014 Ahmed Miqdad

All rights reserved.

ISBN-13: 978-1502940612

ISBN-10: 1502940612

Cover Photograph by Khaled El Sabah

PREFACE

Gaza is the symbol of suffering and pain. It represents oppressed people all over the world. It is the city of martyrs and wounds, the land of homelessness and rubble. Gaza is the slogan for freedom and peace against the occupiers. It suffers from the latest occupation of this world, with an unbearable siege being imposed on the people of Gaza for decades. Gaza encounters big troubles and barriers engineered by the Israeli occupation in order to prevent the Gazans from living peacefully and freely. The crises in Gaza, like a cluster of grapes, are not limited nor are they uncounted. For example, the power, water, fuel, transportation, unemployment, and so on, with every aspect of life included.

It is so worthy to write about Gaza and it deserves notice from all people worldwide. It is our right as Palestinians to write our feelings about the misery of Gaza and show the whole world what the Israeli occupation is doing against innocent Palestinians. We have to use all different types of writing to express the suffering of the Gazans and to expose the Israeli genocide toward the children, women, and old people. Writing demonstrates the various images of the Israeli aggression in Gaza, and it illustrates with clear descriptions of the scenes in Gaza.

My poetry is a means to achieve the freedom of my people and help the whole world understand about Gaza city. In addition, it narrates the suffering of my people and the crimes committed by the Israelis in Palestine, especially Gaza city. I try to draw the images using the words of my poems to show the real suffering and miserable conditions of the Palestinian people because of the Israeli occupation. I do my best to be close to the reality of life in Gaza city, and to make the western people more aware of the suffering of the Palestinians, the atrocities, and the collective punishment against Gaza city and its people.

I wrote these poems from all aspects of life, especially the suffering, the feelings, the worries, the fears, the rights, and the resistance against the occupation. I tried to use the appropriate words and phrases to express the truth and the real image of the Israeli occupation. Moreover, I expressed my feelings toward the world and the silence of the Arabs, human rights associations, and the western governments that sing and raise the slogans of democracy and freedom.

We would like to use all legal means to bring the rights back to the Palestinians. It is known that where there is an occupation, resistance is a duty. We will resist with weapons and pens, with papers and words. We have the right to defend our land, children, homes and our right to live like all humans on this planet. My only way to fight against the Israeli occupation is the writing of my poetry, it is a peaceful instrument and I am sure it will make people recognize and experience for themselves the hard life of the Palestinians. It will encourage people to demand rights for the Palestinians, to demonstrate in the streets, to boycott Israel in all aspects, and to make people more aware of the Palestinian cause and the Israeli atrocities we have been suffering for more than 66 years. I hope my poems will deliver the message that it carries between the lines and describe the scandal of Israeli crimes against the innocents and the civilians in Gaza.

I wrote my poems through the latest war on Gaza which started in July, 2014 and lasted for fifty-one days. I wrote them under the shelling and attacks of the Israeli planes and tanks, under the hovering of the drones and the sounds of rockets and heavy bombs, between the homeless civilians and between my little children. I wrote these poems, with the lack of power and food, and with fear and stress. These poems were written from my heart to the heart of my reader.

I hope you like my poems and understand the messages in them. Then you can show your support as a human being to the Palestinian cause. I hope the reader will enjoy reading this book of poems that describes the suffering of innocent people in Gaza. Please spread the word about this book, and recommend your friends read it.

DEDICATION

For the sake of Allah, my Creator and my Master,
My great teacher and messenger, Mohammed (May Allah bless and reward him), who taught us the purpose of life,
My homeland Palestine, the warmest womb,
My city Gaza, the symbol of dignity,
The Palestinian resistance, who defend land and honor,
The great martyrs and prisoners, the symbol of sacrifice,
The wounded who paid their blood cheaply for Palestine,
The homeless in the streets of Gaza,

My great parents, who never stop giving of themselves in countless ways,

My dearest wife, who leads me through the valley of darkness with her light of hope and support,

My beloved brothers and sisters, the symbol of respect,

My beloved kids Dana and Kareem, whom I could never force myself to stop loving.

To all my family, the symbol of love and giving,

My friends who encourage and support me, especially Magdalena and Nisfa,

To all the people in my life who touch my heart, I dedicate this book.

CONTENTS

	Acknowledgments	i
1	Gaza is Burning	1
2	Gaza is Pure	5
3	I was Lying to You	7
4	I Will Always Remember You	9
5	I Miss My Village	11
6	Palestine	13
7	Dialogue Between Me and My Mind	15
8	Tale of a Prisoner	17
9	Be Careful	19
10	Eid in Gaza	21
11	Silence is Everywhere	25
12	No Way to Escape	29
13	Dove of Peace	31
14	The Lovely Bell	33

CONTENTS....2

15	Til the Last Drop	33
16	The Key	37
17	War of 2008	39
18	We are Humans	41
19	We Lost our Flowers	45
20	We Will All Cry For You Mohammed	47
21	We Will Never Surrender	49
22	Where Am I From?	51
23	The Orphan - Gaza	53
24	Since I Was Born	55
25	The Sun Will Rise	57
26	Between Day and Night	59
27	Resist to Exist	61
28	A leg or a Heart?	63
29	Gaza Won	65

ACKNOWLEDGMENTS

In the Name of Allah, the Most Merciful, the Most Compassionate all praise be to Allah, the Lord of the worlds; and prayers and peace be upon Mohammed His servant and messenger.

First and foremost, I must acknowledge my limitless thanks to Allah, the Ever-Magnificent; the Ever-Thankful, for His help and blessings. I am entirely certain that this work would never have been realized without His guidance.

I owe a deep debt of gratitude to my city and my refugee camp for inspiring me to write this book.

I am grateful to the people who worked hard with me from the beginning till the completion of this work, particularly my dear sisters Magdalena and the two photographers Heba Kraizem and Khaled Al-Sabah, who never stopped giving me their support and encouragement. In addition, my deep thanks to all my friends who made recommendations and suggestions, notably Hank Lawler and Mohammed Al-Amodi. Also to my kind friends Marsha Lougue, Sarah, Nuriyya McKee and Esther Weatley, who have helped me with editing and arranging.

I would like to take this opportunity to offer my warm thanks to all my beloved friends who have been so supportive along the way.

I would also like to express my wholehearted thanks to my family for the generous support they have provided me throughout my entire life. Because of their unconditional love and prayers, I now have the chance to complete this book.

I owe profound gratitude to my wife, Amal, whose constant encouragement, limitless giving and great sacrifice helped me accomplish my degree.

Last but not least, my deepest thanks go to all the people who took part in making this project a reality.

GAZA IS BURNING

No place is safe,
Every place is attacked,
No time for targeting,
Every minute, a bomb here and another there,
Gaza is bleeding,
Children are so afraid,
Mothers are crying for mercy,
Fathers are sleepless,
Trying to take care of their families,
So many martyred,
Red blood covers the bodies,
A lot of wounded,
Deeply broken cracks, bodies shredded,
And the world is dead,
No voice,
No action,
What are you waiting for??!!
The number of martyrs is not enough,
The broken bodies in the streets are not seen,
What are the required numbers to move?
The Arab world is absent in this drama,
The West is busy with the Zionist media,
What they hear is,
A rocket from Gaza falls in Israel,
Then thousands of tons of explosives,
Rain as fireworks on Gaza,
No wounds and no martyrs in Israel,
Children are afraid to sleep,
Nothing should move during day and night,

AHMED MIQDAD

War planes raid from the sky,
Warships attack from the sea,
Artillery targets from a faraway land,
Israel is pouring the lava on Gaza,
Massive explosions shake our homes,
Huge sounds wake up the dead,
Empty areas are attacked,
Homes fall on the residents,
A child becomes just body parts,
While he is playing with a ball,
A woman dies,
Thinking, it's safe to eat,
A father is attacked,
While he is gathering food,
Drones are watching the whole day long,
No one is safe,
The political leaders are watching,
That one feels sympathy with Israelis,
And the other condemns the rockets from Gaza,
And the rest takes rest,
Are they humans while we are not?!!,
You shouldn't be blind or see with one eye,
See the real image without bias,
We hate killing but,
We must act with resistance,
We resist to gain our legal rights,
To live peacefully, move safely,
Everyone is talking about human rights,
Where are human rights for the Palestinians?!
They are humans like any others,
The united nations are dying,
Hundreds of martyrs are nothing,
Yet one Israeli is unacceptable,

GAZA NARRATES POETRY

The chosen people are criminals,

Killing every hope and wish,
Destroying their homes and farms,
Burn the bodies of our martyred,
Eradicate their trees from the land,
This is allowed, yet,
We are not allowed to defend ourselves,
What unfair law do you follow,
That Occupation is legal,?
And the occupied must surrender,
Gaza is burning,
Uncounted attacks to report,
People are running in the streets,
Mothers searching for their children,
All are afraid of bombs,
Earthquakes hit Gaza,
Keep your children close to you,
Gather the whole family in one safe room,
Sorry, the Israeli rocket is strong heavy enough,
To destroy the building and reach that room,
But stay strong with faith,
Allah will protect you,
The smell of death, the odor,
The scenes of killing like in an action film,
Unbelievable scenes, but they are real,
We feel the pain and wounds,
We have blood in our veins,
We are all martyrs,
But we wait for the role,
We will be the curse,
That chases the Israelis,
The day will come,
We will revenge our children, mothers, and fathers,

AHMED MIQDAD

Be ready, we will not show mercy, but wrath,

Gaza is burning,
Is there any action that will stop this atrocity,
Or just condemn us as usual.

GAZA IS PURE

Gaza is like an honored legend,
One day the invaders came,
Attacked the virgin city,
Women were in their homes,
Taking care of their children,
Engaged with home work,
Men were away in the fields,
Irrigating the trees,
Collecting the wheat,
Strangers raped the women,
They lost their honor,
And held the shame,
Gathered and talked,
What the strangers made!,
Suddenly, they remembered,
An absent woman called Gaza,
She was not with the ladies,
Let's go and see,
The solider might kill her,
Or be unable to move,
It was surprising,
She opened the door,
A coward dead soldier,
Pulling the soldier out,
We thought you were killed!!,
I killed that stranger,
How dare you?!,
Let strangers take your honor,
Before you protect and fight for,
Where are your dead ones?!!,

AHMED MIQDAD

Ladies were conspiring and plotting,
Let's kill Gaza,
She will tell our men,
Then, they attacked and killed her,
Like Arabs lost their honor,
And conspired on Gaza,
They sold their honor,
And bought shame instead.
We live with honor,
And die without shame.

GAZA NARRATES POETRY

I WAS LYING TO YOU

When she was so young,
I used to lie to her,
I don't want her to be afraid,
I say, don't worry my daughter,
They are sounds from a near party,
While the Israeli jets are attacking,
When she got older,
Don't be afraid my daughter,
Such sounds are far away from us,
Are they fireworks, Dad?!!
No parties and no new year,
But every night was a new life for us,
These are the Israeli bombs my young one,
Do you enjoy them like fireworks?,
They are so disturbing and noisy dad,
You should know that,
These are not games to play nor a celebration,
These are the gifts of your enemy,
Your small body is vulnerable,
One bullet is enough,
Such sounds aren't musical tones,
They are able to deafen your ears,
And split your soft body into pieces,
Do you remember that day?,
When you covered your head with your pillow,
Huge explosions around us,
My daughter, remember,
With every sound, innocents die,
Mothers, fathers, children, no matter,

AHMED MIQDAD

My daughter, remember,
With every shake of our home,
Many homes fall down on the innocents' heads,
My daughter, remember,
This is the truth about that,
My daughter, remember,
To forgive me because I was lying to you.

I WILL ALWAYS REMEMBER YOU

I will always remember you,
When I open my eyes after a dark night,
Full of hope that you have returned back home,
I will always remember you,
When the dawn knocks deep in the night,
With a hope your jail is getting tired,
I will always remember you,
When the sun rises,
With its ray of light in your cell,
I will always remember you,
When the news mentions the prisoners,
I will always remember you,
When I smell your clothes,
I will always remember you,
When I see your empty bed,
I will always remember you,
When your children are around me,
I will always remember you,
When the youngest says papa,
I will always remember you,
When I look into the eyes of your father,
I will always remember you,
When our door opens,
I will always remember you,
When I see the birds fly,
I will always remember you,
When everyone is here without you,
I will always remember you,
When I cover your brothers without you,

AHMED MIQDAD

I will always remember you,
When I hear a voice saying Allah u Akbar,
I will always remember you,
When the church bells ring,
I will always remember you,
When we are gathered around the table,
And your chair is empty,
I will always remember you,
With every beat of my heart,
I will always remember you,
With every breathe I take,
I will always remember you.

GAZA NARRATES POETRY

I MISS MY VILLAGE

I miss my village,
My father was born there,
As my grandfather was before,
My mother was born in that simple home,
I wake up in another city,
It is a city of my country,
But it is not the village of my ancestors,
They made us leave by force,
They destroyed our homes,
Killed our ancestors,
I used to go to the north,
A high hill is close to borders,
Near the beach by the sea,
Look to the far north,
Where the north west winds blow,
Smell the grapes,
The fish swim there,
The beautiful fields,
All that was stolen,
I wish I could be there,
But this would cost me my soul,
I miss you my village,
One day I will kiss your white sands,
And the occupiers will pay the price,
I miss you, " Hamama village"

AHMED MIQDAD

PALESTINE

I'm the mother of all martyrs,
I'm the healer of all wounds,
I'm the keeper of the widows,
It's me, the sponsor of the sacred places,
I'm the mother of all orphans,
My body, so full of patriotism,
My veins are red rivers of blood,
Water, the convoy of martyrs,
My streets witness the shredded bodies,
My cities live the old memories,
The memories of Israeli wars,
I'm the land of olive trees,
I'm the land of green fields,
I'm well-known for my oranges,
It's me, starting from the sea,
At my end is a river,
I stretch from the green farms north,
To the desert south,
I teach my children to love me more than themselves,
I infuse the taste of sacrifice in their souls,
To present them for my sake,
I raise my children to fight my enemies,
I feed freedom and dignity to their hearts,
The letters of my name indicate to me,

AHMED MIQDAD

"P" peace and peace,
"A" refers to a lot of patience,
"L" means limitless love,
"E" is for all eternity,
"S" denotes our solidarity,
"T" indicates my tolerance,
"I" I love you,
"N" Needy for you,
"E" is enormous freedom,
It's me, Palestine.

GAZA NARRATES POETRY

DIALOGUE BETWEEN ME AND MY MIND

One black night,
The moon is far away in the sky,
No more lights,
Silence is everywhere,
News is so urgent,
More martyrs and wounds,
Demolished homes in rubble ,
No one is in the streets,
Drones and many jets in the sky,
Sounds of bombs so loud,
Explosions everywhere,
The screaming of mothers and kids,
Crying of father and sons,
Waiting the new role to come,
My mind is so busy thinking,
Planning for ways to escape,
Mind suggests different strategies,
Once I will be a superhero,
Will be able to protect family,
Will save the lives of kids,
Like an action movie,
I will be the hero,
Then wake up,
Think more realistic,
How could I face this?!,
A big bomb with wide destruction,
Kids will be small pieces,
Homes layers will become,
Like a sandwich biscuit,

AHMED MIQDAD

Rocks will grind the bodies,
Try not to think anymore about it,
Stop my mind from thinking of,
Another time when ,
The sounds of planes appear,
Imagine if a rocket comes through the window,
I will face it with my body,
Keep my wife and kids safe,
I will die so that they live,
My soul is cheap,
For the sake of my family,
Shall my kids be orphans?!
No, my mind says,
Think of something else,
Shall we stay so close?!,
Live together or die together,
No one to mourn the other,
So sad a tragedy,
Stop my mind from imagining this,
Could you suggest something else?!,
My mind replies sadly,
So sorry,
No more choices available,
So, you, you , you,
Can you recommend another way?!

GAZA NARRATES POETRY

TALE OF A PRISONER

Days and days,
Months and months,
Years and years,
Such a long time ago,
I forgot the date,
What I remember is that,
I was twenty-two years old,
During a cloudy night,
Full of strong winds and heavy rains,
The door knocked like thunder,
I was ordered to get out of my home,
Leave my parents, wife, kids, and family,
Take off your clothes this one said,
Bind his hands he shouted,
Cover his eyes the officer said,
I open my eyes with the new dawn,
Find myself in an Israeli jail,
I became like a bird in a cage,
So sad for that bird because I taste it,
They kept me in my cage,
Then investigations and torture,
No accusations or a sentence,
You will be an administrative prisoner,
Their justice pronounced,
Two years will be renewed depending on the circumstances,
Two years, two years, then two years more,
Days come and go while I contact family through letters,
I wish to kiss my parents' hands,
Cuddle my kids in my arms,

AHMED MIQDAD

the forehead of my wife for her patience,
My freedom is like the light at the end of the tunnel,
When it comes so close,
They renew my sentence,
My guilt is I'm a Palestinian,
My soul, body, kids, and all,
Everything is priceless for Palestine,
My wish is to see,
My Palestine free.

GAZA NARRATES POETRY

BE CAREFUL

Be careful when the night comes,
The sound of the cockroaches is clear,
The calm before the storm,
Be careful when the sky is pure,
The winds are not so strong,
The stars are glamorous,
Nice weather and the party will start,
Be careful when the drones fly,
They are like flies on a corpse,
They monitor the innocent Gazans,
They attack with small rockets,
Such missiles are so effective,
Full of needles and pins,
With sharp and killing iron pieces,
Be careful when the black owls come,
They appear with bright eyes during night,
They used to appear at that time,
No sounds of such warplanes,
Till the explosion happened,
Shakes homes like an earthquake,
Huge damage in the near homes,
Broken windows with cracks,
Fear all over the area,
Crying of the kids and women,
Be careful for you are in Gaza,
Unexpected attacks,
No date and no time,
A man on a motorbike might be attacked,
A car nearby might be targeted,

AHMED MIQDAD

A family on the beach might be shot,
An extreme sound here, or that,
A friend might fall near you,
The smell of death is everywhere,
If you are alive during day,
You are not sure of the night,
Death is so close to us,
Closer than our own shadows,
Be careful when you encounter people who,
Have been Obliged to leave their lands,
Sacrifice by thousands of martyrs,
Lost everything beautiful,
Have nothing to cry for,
Face soldiers with bare bodies,
Fight for their legal and basic rights,
Be careful when the Palestinian giant wakes up,
They will eradicate the occupation,
And restore this land and freedom.

EID IN GAZA

In which case you come,
How shall We celebrate you?!!,
Happiness is gone and under rubble,
Joy is buried in many tombs,
Tears are shed from the eyes,
Screaming is heard everywhere,
Smiles have been deleted from the dictionary,
Blood covers the streets,
Smell of death is inside homes,
Bodies are still being collected,
In which case you come,
How shall we celebrate you?!!,
More and more martyrs,
Thousands of wounded in beds,
Blood, still bleeding,
Bombs are everywhere,
Drones fly so close,
Kids die without guilt of the killer,
Elderly pass away each moment,
Mothers leave their families,
In which case you come,
How shall we celebrate you?!!,
Homes are demolished,
Mosques are targeted,
Hospitals are attacked,
People mourn their loved ones,
Streets are damaged beyond recognition,
Smell of blood is so fresh,
Relatives are at schools,
Children have no new clothes,

AHMED MIQDAD

Sweets are not bought,

In which case you come,
How shall we celebrate you?!!,
Smell of coffee fills the air,
Only coffee is available with dates,
Funerals are in every street,
Children are so afraid,
Don't go out of your homes,
Lost kids are still lost,
Martyrs are under remains of buildings,
Pain of wounded in hospitals,
In which case you come,
How shall we celebrate you?!!,
Fathers are crying,
Mothers are fainting,
Sisters are mourning,
Brothers are heartbroken,
Relatives gather to comfort each other,
Sons are weeping,
Daughters are so sad,
Families accept condolences,
Neighbors are so compassionate,
In which case you come,
How shall we celebrate you?!!,
Lovers are in their hearts,
Memories are remembered,
Martyrs images etched in our minds,
Wives are missing their husbands,
Kids are waiting for their dead fathers,

Homes are missing,
A father or a mother,
A son or a daughter,
Or all have gone,
No toys and no games,
In which case you come,
How shall we celebrate you?!!.

AHMED MIQDAD

GAZA NARRATES POETRY

SILENCE IS EVERYWHERE

When the sun disappears,
Away behind the sea,
The moon is far away in the sky,
No more light,
Gaza is so afraid,
No more voices cry out,
The streets are empty,
Kids cling to their mothers,
The elders are inside their homes,
Looking for a safe place,
Cars are stopped,
No more movement,
Silence is everywhere,
A weak light from candles,
Just see how to move,
No lights in the near homes,
No sight is available,
Everything is black outside,
Stay near the kids,
That They might feel secure,
You are an old father,
You are the source of safety,
Hide your fear in front of kids,
Pretend you are the protector,
But if someone looks inside your heart,
The Fear is enough for the whole world,
Fathers are awake all night,
Ready to cuddle the one who cries,
That one might shout,

AHMED MIQDAD

Check they are all covered,
From cold and fear,
Silence is everywhere,
All the neighbors are sleeping,
The sounds of laughter and noise,
Omitted from the agenda,
The drones are just out,
The smell of death,
Outside the doors,
The ghost of darkness,
Inside the homes,
Zzzzzzzzz ennnnnnnn,
The sound of drones,
Make hearts beat strongly,
Boooooom, booooom,
The sounds of huge bombs,
Shake the homes,
The crying kids at night,
The fear of mothers,
That breaks the silence,
Nothing else you could do,
Sitting beside your kids,
Waiting the day,
You pray the sun is up,
And tell the kids a story,
To help them sleep,
A story talks about dignity and freedom,
It is full of hope and positives,
And at the end,
A promise,
That the dawn of freedom will appear,
Fill them with hope,

That freedom is so close,
Like the period,
Between night and day,
It comes from far away,
That far tunnel,
Light and hope is at the end,
While silence is everywhere.

AHMED MIQDAD

NO WAY TO ESCAPE

So dark is the night,
There is no light,
Faces full of stress and concerns,
Worries and internal pressures,
Sounds of explosions,
Military lanterns,
Shows of yellow light,
Smell of death,
Comes out of it,
More anxiety and fear,
Such light is a sign of danger,
This Area will be targeted,
Are you ready ?!,
Gather the family,
Hold tight to the children,
A safe room in the middle of the house,
Think how to escape,
Evacuate the children,
Shall I start with,
The youngest or the oldest,
Will we all die?,
And no one mourns the others,
Or a part of ,
To save lives,
There is no time,
The bombs come so quick,
Should throw them out of windows,
They might have a chance,
To stay alive as handicapped,
Better than being shredded bodies,
Shall we all sleep,

To die makes no sense,
Shall keep them under stairs,
They might survive,
Get them out from the rubble,
Each floor of my home,
Will collapse,
Each floor will,
Grind my babies soft bodies,
Where shall we escape to?!!
Streets are so empty,
No cats or dogs,
Drones are overhead, hovering,
They are all so afraid,
My small birds,
Stay inside their nest,
Weak sounds they murmur,
Look at me with sad eyes,
So afraid are their pale faces,
The whites are sorrowful,
They Tell the tale of,
Patience and hope,
They Appeal to me, take them out,
As a part of the family,
A glimmer of light with silence,
Just the blasts break it,
We Shall stay and wait,
Death knocks on the doors,
We Prefer to die together,
And be satisfied with our destiny,
We Accept our fate,
To Either stay alive,
Or die under the rubble,
Just read Quran and say our prayers,
The sounds gently fall on our soft bodies,
And Over our peaceful souls.

DOVE OF PEACE

My lovely white dove,
Shall I see you in my home?,
It's been a long time,
And I have been waiting you,
With every new day,
My hope increases for things to come,
With each new night,
My dreams are about you,
Your whiteness inspires me with hope,
Your wings demonstrate the meaning of freedom,
The olive branch predicts the beautiful days,
You will bring with you,
I have been waiting for you for a long time,
Don't you want come?!,
Be sure, I'm waiting for you on pins and needles,
I suffer enough please come for me,
I'm so jealous when I see you fly freely,
Come and take me with you,
It is me, Palestine,
The one who deserves peace,
My martyrs' blood irrigates the olive trees,
Come and take my olive branch,
And give me your peace,
I'm waiting you my lovely dove.

AHMED MIQDAD

THE LOVELY BELL

What an incredible bell?!
What amazing sounds?!
What beautiful musical notes?!!
You are my lovely bell,
Giving hope after so much despair,
Shows the light after darkness,
So Take a deep breath,
When it rings,
Give life after death,
I miss you my lovely bell,
No more rings for so long,
Are you disappearing default?!
Miss your nice sound,
That beautiful sound,
I am still waiting to hear,
Want to meet my friends,
Need to do some business,
We are so bound to you,
So durable is the relationship,
Very close friends,
Always pay attention,
With hope to hear you,
But it all was in vain,
At that far home in my town,
You live as my neighbor,
And I miss you like,
A lover misses his fiancée,
I miss you like,
A prisoner misses his freedom,
I miss you like,

AHMED MIQDAD

The darkness misses light,
I miss you like,
The thirsty misses water,
You are the one who,
Gives light all around,
You are the one who,
Provides me with power,
But the news says,
You will not ring anymore,
For a year or more,
You will be silent,
The occupiers don't want,
To hear your sound,
They want the darkness,
To cover all of Gaza,
That remote bell,
With so strong a sound,
To wake people,
To indicate that,
Power is available now,
No more singing for power,
We hope to hear your sounds,
Even After a year,
But I will await you,
Till you ring again,
And give us hope and light.

TIL THE LAST DROP

In spite of the hard life in Gaza,
The hovering of war planes,
The missiles from war ships,
The bullets of heavy and light weapons,
The rockets of blind drones,
The massive attacks on us,
The huge explosions on our land,
The noisy sound of F16 planes,
The tons of explosives against our bodies,
We will remain Till the last drop,
Although the big number of martyrs,
The unlimited wounds,
The crying of our babies,
The screaming of our women,
The fear inside our hearts,
The mutilated bodies on the streets,
The rubble of our homes,
The blood all over Gaza,
The tears of our parents,
Till the last drop,
We will never give up,
We will never surrender,
We will fight,
Till the last drop.

AHMED MIQDAD

THE KEY

She is an old lady called Palestine,
I used to see her crying eyes,
With a bleeding heart like a continuous river,
A big key on a necklace around her neck,
I wonder why it's such an old and rusty key,
There are no more doors with locks for those keys,
I smell the leaves of grapes,
I breathe the air of my villages,
I taste the oranges of my fields,
After years and years,
She says this key must be kept safe,
Till the day of our return comes.

AHMED MIQDAD

WAR OF 2008

Am I dreaming and my dream was a nightmare?!!
Sounds of knocking on the door of my room,
More and more blasts and they become louder,
Suddenly, several blasts hit and I jump up like a crazy man,
Open my window to see the destruction, papers flying everywhere,
The sky is full of dust and ash,
The smell of smoke, bombs in the air,
All the people below me in the streets,
It was like dooms day,
I see a man, he goes to check on his family,
Another asks for his kids,
The other goes to bring his child from school,
I look and see the heavy smoke all over Gaza,
Turn on the radio for more news,
Countless number of martyrs already dead,
Hospitals are so crowded with wounded ,
That was the first day,
Each day of that war was like a year,
If the day is up, you wish night comes,
And if the night comes, you wish the day appears,
The whole family sleeps in the same room,
Stay away from the windows,
Do not use light during night,
Sleep close to your children,
Do not go out at night,
Drones like black birds in the sky,
Warships line the shore,
F16 and helicopters hovering over you,
No need to listen to news,

No one knows the targets,
One of the nights was like a red hell,
The room is so black,
Sit down and wait for the rocket,
Constant explosions,
Sounds of the raiding planes,
I thought I was the only one who was still alive in my area,
I expect to have to bury my neighbors,
The smell of phosphorus around the area,
demolished homes, burning kids, more blood,
More than a thousand and five hundred dead,
Most of them women and children,
We will investigate the Israeli crimes,
It was the end of that war.

WE ARE HUMANS

We are humans,
Wish to live peacefully,
Seek to have a stable country,
Ask for legal rights,
Need to be secured,
We are humans,
So afraid of killing,
Wish for a beautiful life,
Be kind with others,
Hope to be like everyone else,
With compassionate hearts,
Want to be appreciated,
We are humans,
Hate aggressors,
Defend our home,
Fight against occupiers,
Look after our freedom,
Need an independent state,
To live freely and peacefully,
We are humans,
Want to move with no checkpoints,
Leave to travel everywhere without obstacles,
Return back at any time,
Have our own harbor and airport,
Work with all the business,
All goods are needed,
No need to stay,
Under the mercy of others,
Egyptians are to the south,
Occupiers are to the north and east,

Sea from the west,
Under the control of the oppressors,
We are humans,
Love all people,
And all love us,
Our kids must have a future,
They will be the leaders,
The horizon should be clear,
To achieve the far reaching goals,
And build our country,
We are humans,
We should not die easily,
Not to shed our blood,
Like rivers in the streets,
Children lose their lives,
Their torn bodies are everywhere,
Mothers leave the kids,
Fathers say farewell to their families,
We are humans,
We have as much dignity as others,
All humans are equal,
None is better than the other,
Americans,
French,
English,
Are not better than Palestinians,
Your kids are not special,
Your mothers are not better than ours,
Your fathers are like ours,
We have feelings and emotions,
We are not goats,
Our souls are not cheap,
Our kids are priceless,
Our blood is high quality,
We are humans,
Why do not humans move?!!

Everyday more people are killed,
Homes are demolished,
Blood flows like a flood,
Atrocities are committed,
Collective punishment, genocides,
Thousands are dying,
Martyrs are under the rubble,
Hospitals are overcrowded,
And they are targeted,
Schools are attacked,
Families leave homes,
No food or clothes,
Innocents with no guilt,
But being Palestinian,
All this is not a motivation,
To help all humanity,
Why do you help?!
When a westerner is abused,
A dog is killed in an accident,
An iceberg melts in the Antarctica,
A mouse is shot in a jungle,
But why do not you move?!
While Palestinians are cleansed,
We are humans,
And no humanity without,
A fair world with all humans,
Especially Palestinians,
Who have lost everything,
Except their humanity.

AHMED MIQDAD

WE LOST OUR FLOWERS

We lost our flowers,
The garden is so fantastic,
The flowers are colorful,
They are getting older,
Day after day,
The gardener watches them,
The wife is so kind,
Don not touch any,
So beautiful and nice,
Take special care of flowers,
We are waiting for the sweet smell ,
They are our kids,
Years after years,
They are getting older,
Others are still so young,
Such weak branches,
Soft leaves,
The weather changed fast,
Clouds of black smoke ,
Storm of bombs is tremendous ,
Such a phenomenon is so weird,
It is raining missiles,
Heavy and massive blasts,
Burn,
Destroy,
Eradicate,
Kill,
The soft leaves were cut,
The weak branches were broken,
Heavy raining and strong wind,

AHMED MIQDAD

Our flowers died,
Such bombs are destructive,
The mother's heart wrenches,
No mercy for the flowers,
Our flowers are our kids,
Every day we lose flowers,
Their smell was so apparent,
The odor of blood,
The blood irrigate the land,
Flowers will come up again,
The enemy must know,
Our flowers will never die,
If you kill one,
We will plant two,
Till the land is free,
And flowers give us,
The smell of our freedom.

WE WILL ALL CRY FOR YOU, MOHAMMED

You are our angel,
Who shows us the straight path,
You are the fire,
With Which we will burn the criminals,
You are the white bird,
Which shows the meaning of innocence,
You are the child,
Who will disgrace the murderers,
You are the martyr,
That will storm the occupation,
You are the hurricane,
That will eradicate the settlers,
You are the blood,
That they will sink in,
You are the lion,
Which will furiously destroy his enemies,
You are the wrath,
That will curse the silent ones,
We will cry for you,
Mohammed, and you will be,
The owner of the land,
Our hero against the occupiers,
The shadow that will chase your killers,
The nightmare that will intrude on their nights,
We will cry for you,
You will be there in the distance,
But your smile will be inside us,
They burn your soft body,
But your soul will fly to heaven,
They put Benz in your mouth,

AHMED MIQDAD

But your fire will be their hell,
They committed a grave crime,
But Allah will judge with fire,
The Most Just and the Most Fair,
Will avenge you,
We will cry for you.

WE WILL NEVER SURRENDER

We will never surrender,
If we strive for victory ,
We will grind the sand to eat,
If we are thirsty,
We will drink the sea water,
If we are homeless,
We will make the earth our beds,
And the sky our blanket,
If all doors are closed,
We will knock on the door of the sky,
If all the trees are cut,
We will plant more and more and more,
If we lose our babies,
We will give birth to thousands more,
We will never surrender,
In spite of the thousands of martyrs,
And the pain of our prisoners' mothers,
The tears of our widows,
The loss of our limbs,
The cries of our wounded,
The pieces of broken bodies,
The rubble of our homes,
The crying of our orphans,
The corpses of our dead bodies,
The sounds of your warplanes,
The sounds of your bombs,
The fear of our children,
We will never surrender,
Although you are the knife,
And we are the flesh,

AHMED MIQDAD

You are the killer,
And we are the murdered,
You are the kidnapper,
And we are the hostages,
You are the oppressor,
And we are the oppressed,
You are the occupier,
And we are the occupied,
You are the strong because of your weapons,
And we are the strong because of our faith,
You are the rock,
And we are the drops,
Drop, drop, drop,
The rock may crack,
But we will never surrender.

WHERE AM I FROM?

My father is from Hamamah,
And Hamamah is a Palestinian village,
Al-Jaleel, Safad, Haifa are Palestinians,
My grandma is from Akka,
And Akka is a Palestinian city,
Al-Ramla, Al-Najab, and Jaffa are Palestinians,
My grandpa is from Bissan,
And Bissan is a Palestinian city,
I am from Gaza,
And Gaza is a Palestinian city,
Palestine is not Israel,
Palestine is the occupied Palestine.

THE ORPHAN - GAZA

I am an orphan,
Although I have many fathers and mothers,
And many, many relatives,
I am an orphan
My fathers left me alone,
For more than sixty years,
They went with no way back,
They slept like the people of the cave,
My mothers are so busy,
With their new husbands,
Involved with their problems,
Husbands are so bad,
They are traitors and collaborators,
Follow their big bosses,
For their interests and benefits,
I am an orphan,
They sold me without price,
Intending to take my nationality,
My kids are killed,
My Sons are martyrs,
Many Thousands are wounded,
Most of the Land is stolen,
Our Trees are cut,
Leaving Many homeless and handicapped,
I am an orphan,
My relatives have passed away,
Arabs are absent,
Humanity is buried,
No morals or honor,
The law of the jungle,

AHMED MIQDAD

The strong devours the weak,
No one dares to speak out loud,
I am an orphan,
But my children will fight,
The land will be ploughed,
The homes will be rebuilt,
Olive trees will be planted,
Nothing will stop me,
If you don't know me,
You can ask about,
The orphan Gaza.

SINCE I WAS BORN

When the dawn cleared the horizon,
And light passed into my eyes,
A small baby screamed loudly,
Send me back to that world,
The world of safety and peace,
The world of love and compassion,
But you were born and there is no going back,
Face your future life,
Life is more beautiful than that world,
You will meet all humanity,
They are all together with no differences,
Love and peace is everywhere,
No fears or worries,
I believed that for so long,
But I was shocked after two years,
The first Intifada started,
Weapons, planes, and bullets,
Soldiers are running while the youth flee,
Red color on the clothes,
Was that a tragic drama?!!
The one who acted was truly killed,
The bullets were real, and so alive,
Blood was not merely painted,
Discovering the real image of life,
After two years of my birth,
Some years later Al-Aqsa Intifada started,
Full evidence of oppression,
Martyrs and wounded,
Arrested, detained in the Israeli jails,
Helicopters were assassinating everyone they saw,

AHMED MIQDAD

Cars were targeted,
Military operations on land,
Confirmed and tied to the siege on Gaza,
Two thousands and six has started,
No more food, or medicines,
No fuel or materials,
The only solution for living,
Tunnel under the borders,
A sudden war has begun,
It was eleven thirty,
People out in the streets,
Living peaceful lives,
Martyrs are everywhere,
An earth quick stroke upon Gaza,
Demolished buildings again,
It was two thousands and eight,
The most savage war we witnessed,
Dozens of warplanes attacked,
Prohibited weapons were used,
Then the war of the eight days,
No safety or peace,
Many homes were attacked,
With heavy missiles and rockets,
Drones were crowded the skies over there,
None moved in the streets,
Waiting for night to come,
Then wishing for day to appear,
Heavy shelling from their tanks,
And ships from the sea,
And the latest war nowadays,
So severe and dangerous,
It is the war of many homes,
Thousands of homes were demolished,
Unlimited numbers of missiles,
Thousands of martyrs,
Ten thousand wounded,

Most of them are children and women,
No power or water,
No homes or shelters,
Fear and worries,
Wait your role until death,
Gather the family to die all together,
Homeless people wait in schools,
Borders are closed,
Everything everywhere destroyed and broken,
Except our willingness and faith,
We are the owners of this land,
And we will win it back one day,
And before my suffering,
And My parents suffering,
I was going to blame them,
But I found the dignity in Gaza,
And we will teach the people,
Lessons of freedom and victory,
I am proud to be born a Palestinian,
And give my sacrifice for the whole misjudged people,
I will Show the most beautiful images of patience,
My children will sacrifice too,
Like father and granddad,
And we will never give up,
Till we have our rights back.

AHMED MIQDAD

THE SUN WILL RISE

The sun will rise,
But now It is so dark,
Blood flows like a flood,
Another martyr, one after another,
Leaving to enter heaven,
The wounded struggle with their pain,
Mosques are calling,
No one responds,
So sad are the faces of parents,
Tears run down their cheeks,
Like a continuous river,
Widows endure their loss,
Sons stand steadfast,
The sun will rise,
The tanks will not erase us,
Tons of explosives are in vain,
We will not be broken,
Planes will not stop the battle,
Missiles and rockets will not,
We will reach the sun of our freedom,
None will ban the sun,
No one will deprive us,
The land will be returned back to us,
Rights will be taken back,
Even your high wall,
The sun will be higher,
And Palestine will kiss,
The sun of freedom and victory,
It will cover the sky,
Its smell will be everywhere,
Especially The Dome Of The Rock,

AHMED MIQDAD

Will be yellow like gold
So do not lose hope,
The sun of freedom will rise.

BETWEEN DAY AND NIGHT

Wish the day turns to light,
With hope and optimism,
It will come with a new mission,
A mission of love and peace,
No more martyred or wounded,
No more Homeless or displaced,
No more Destruction or rubble,
It will come with hope,
No more mothers' tears,
No more crying of men,
No more screaming of the children,
Or weeping of widows,
No pain of the wounded,
And torn bodies in the streets,
It will come with a new sunrise,
Bringing freedom and love,
Peace and tranquility,
Not with chaos and terrible sounds,
Tons of explosives and bombs,
And wishing during the night for cover,
The suffering and pain,
Bury the images of destruction,
Erase the miserable conditions,
Remove the tears of wives,
And the blood of bodies,
Wishing night would come,
With love and silence,
With peace and compassion,
Rest and quietness,
Night is created for this,

AHMED MIQDAD

No more attacks and targets,
No more fear and worry,
No more danger and stress,
No more homeless living in the schools,
Hoping night will come,
With peace and freedom,
After the darkness and sadness,
Hope that night will bring,
A new day of freedom,
Peace and love.

RESIST TO EXIST

We will resist,
Whatever this will cost,
Years of suffering,
Compulsory immigration from land,
Unfair laws and agreements,
Blind world without vision,
Brothers left us alone,
Strangers are careless,
We will resist,
Although hundreds are martyred,
Thousands of wounded,
Dozens of widows,
Thousands of orphans,
Large Groups of homeless people,
Pieces of bodies,
Hills of rubble,
Rivers of blood,
We will resist,
Though the destruction is massive,
The killing of olive trees,
The demolishing of homes,
The killing of entire families,
The genocide of children,
The atrocities against the elderly,
We will resist,
In spite of miserable conditions,
The screaming of mothers,
The crying of fathers,
The tears of kids,
The funerals of friends,

AHMED MIQDAD

The farewell of relatives,
The corpses of Palestinians,
We will resist,
Although heavy attacks abound,
The various targets,
The destructive tanks,
The hovering planes,
The flying drones,
The killing missiles,
The prohibited weapons,
The inhuman behavior,
We will resist,
As it was said by the famous,
I think,
I exist,
And we say,
We resist,
Because we exist,
We will resist,
To exist.

A LEG OR A HEART?

The smell of blood is everywhere,
It covers my body with its odor,
The red color waters the clothes and sand,
My old white jacket is red,
The deep wounds kill me,
The unbearable pain has me faint,
My cut leg is bleeding continuously,
No paramedics or bandages,
Unable to move from that place,
Near my destroyed home,
Far away from people,
Rubble covers my body,
My family are all dead,
Gaze at my children,
Then I got faint,
Woke up again,
My wife is on the other side,
Then I lost my awareness,
Unable to help myself,
Or check on my dead family,
I felt so cold,
My body loses blood,
So difficult to take a breath,
So dizzy and sleepy,
Like a mountain over my eyelashes,
None see us under the debris,
I was in a tomb,
But I was alive,
Waiting for the moment of death,
Sun rays passes through a small hole,

Then the sun went far away,
The darkness attacked the place,
I cannot see my family,
Then stay quiet waiting for death,
It was my wish,
To go there with them,
A red siren shows light through the hole,
I hear a voice screaming,
Is there anyone alive?
Is there anyone alive?
I cannot reply to him,
He was about to leave,
But I shouted " Yes, help",
He returned and put the torch in the hole,
He saw me and said be calm,
We will dig and remove the rubble,
I found myself laying on the hospital bed,
Shall you treat my lost leg?
Or shall you cure my broken heart for losing my whole family?
I can live without a leg or two,
But cannot live without my heart.

GAZA WON

Gaza won,
After long days and nights,
Full of fears and worries,
Busy with the martyred and wounded martyrs and wounds,
Homeless people everywhere,
Lacks of medicine and materials,
Complete destruction of homes,
Hospitals and parks,
The homes are only debris,
Suburbs were erased,
A ghost town,
Blood on the earth,
Mixed with sands,
Corpses on the pavements,
Cars were demolished,
Children were burnt,
Gaza won,
Because o0f thousands of martyrs,
Ten thousands injured,
Hundreds of thousands displaced at schools,
Dozens of handicapped and disabled,
Pieces of flying flesh,
Black smoke in the air,
Prohibited gases were used,
Heavy bombs have fallen,
Massive destruction everywhere,
The tons of explosives,
Killing planes were flying,
Different types of drones,
Chasing kids and babies,

AHMED MIQDAD

Rockets targeted infant and the pregnant,

Gaza won,
Although the world is blind,
Full of unfair laws,
More dead Arabs,
The conspiracies of friends,
The plots of the enemies,
The collaboration of spies,
The closed borders,
The support of many weapons,
The many piles of money,
The biased United Nations,
The disabled associations,
Gaza won,
After fifty-one days of war,
By the faith of The Almighty,
The martyrs of her sons,
The patience of Palestinians,
The steadfastness of resistance,
The sincerest of love,
The strongest mothers and fathers,
The tears of the children,

The curses of the widows,
The suffering of daughters,
The pains of the wounded,
The mourning of relatives,
The convoys of martyrs,
The screaming of Gaza,
Gaza won.

NOTES

I had the great pleasure of meeting Ahmed and his family during a trip to Gaza in 2013. They invited me into their house and shared dinner with me. As I played with their beautiful children I was humbled by their generosity and spirit under occupation as Ahmed explained how the occupation affected families every single day. At the time I made a promise to return to Gaza the following year and do whatever I could to help raise awareness about Gaza

Little did I know there would be a second attack on Gaza the following year.

Unfortunately the situation in Gaza makes it extremely difficult for internationals to return to Gaza. Humanitarian help is restricted and the situation worsens daily.

In the meantime it is my pleasure and duty to help to get the book out to the rest of the world

Sarah Strudwick

Made in United States
North Haven, CT
18 July 2022